UNDER WATER

The **TOTALLY AWESOME** guide to **ANIMALS**

By Brenda McHale

BookLife PUBLISHING

©2023
BookLife Publishing Ltd.
King's Lynn
Norfolk, PE30 4LS, UK

All rights reserved.
Printed in Poland.

A catalogue record for this book is available from the British Library.

ISBN: 978-1-80155-651-4

Written by:
Brenda McHale

Edited by:
Emilie Dufresne

Designed by:
Dan Scase

All facts, statistics, web addresses and URLs in this book were verified as valid and accurate at time of writing. No responsibility for any changes to external websites or references can be accepted by either the author or publisher.

PHOTO CREDITS

All images are courtesy of Shutterstock.com. With thanks to Getty Images, Thinkstock Photo and iStockphoto. Front page – saulty72, Damsea. 1 – saulty72. 4&5 – Neel Adsul, wildestanimal, Ernie Hounshell, Jiang Zhongyan, Dan Kosmayer. 6&7 – frantisekhojdysz, Andaman. 8&9 – Steven L. Gordon, Vojce. 10&11 – Ewa Studio, photobeps, James Webb, Adam Ke. 12&13 – Tory Kallman, Neirfy, chonlasub woravichan. 14&15 – Vladimir Wrangel, Yellow Cat, ND700. 16&17 – Sophon K, Eric Isselee, Vladimir Wrangel, Malgorzata Litkowska. 18&19 – Gerald Robert Fischer, Kristina Vackova. 20&21 – Chase Dekker, Andrew Sutton. 22&23 – wildestanimal. Background on all pages – Damsea.

CONTENTS

PAGE 4	What Lives under the Water?
PAGE 6	Wobbegong
PAGE 8	Seahorse
PAGE 10	Starfish
PAGE 12	Dolphin
PAGE 14	Octopus
PAGE 16	Jellyfish
PAGE 18	Pistol Shrimp
PAGE 19	Peacock Mantis Shrimp
PAGE 20	Blue Whale
PAGE 22	Narwhal
PAGE 24	Glossary and Index

Words that look like this can be found in the glossary on page 24.

WHAT LIVES UNDER THE WATER?

Some of the weirdest creatures on our planet live under water. Here are some of the types of animals you can find there...

Fish such as sharks

Mammals such as walruses

Invertebrates such as squid

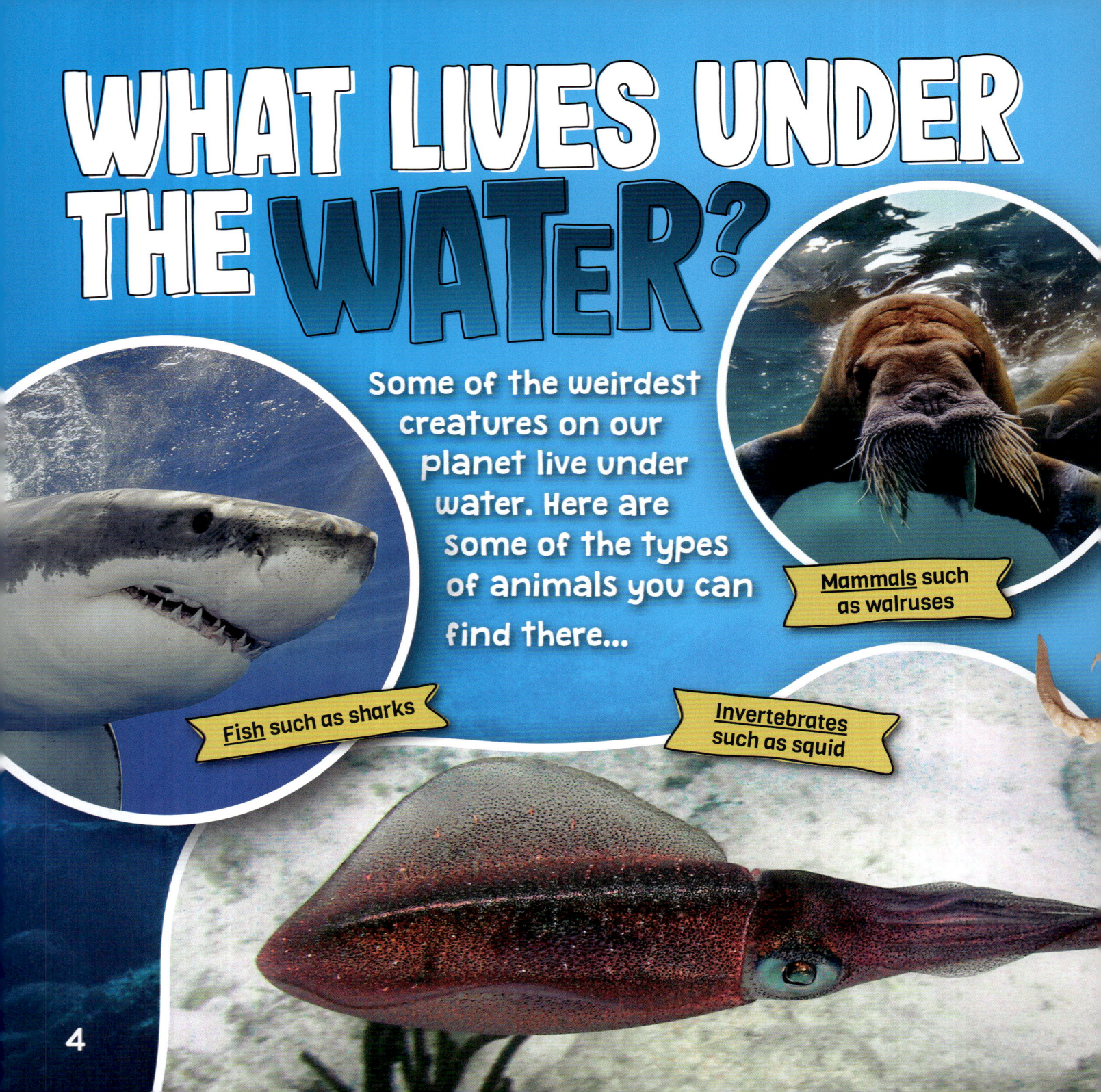

On each page you will see a fact file like this. It will tell you lots of things about the animal, such as what type of animal it is, its <u>diet</u> and where it lives.

SQUID

Type: Invertebrate (mollusc)
Found: Worldwide
Diet: Fish and crustaceans

WOBBEGONG

WOBBEGONG

Type: Vertebrate (fish)
Found: Pacific Ocean and Indian Ocean
Diet: Fish, octopuses and crustaceans

The wobbegong is a type of shark. It is sometimes called the carpet shark.

The wobbegong lies on the sea floor like a shaggy rug. It sneaks up on creatures that come near it.

The tasselled wobbegong has tassels on its face that look like a beard.

A wobbegong's tassels and spotty pattern help it to be camouflaged at the bottom of the ocean.

It can open its mouth very wide very quickly to suck in fish and crustaceans as they swim past.

SEAHORSE

SEAHORSE

Type: Vertebrate (fish)

Found: Warm and temperate waters

Diet: Small crustaceans

Seahorses sometimes like to swim in pairs with their tails linked, as though they are holding hands.

They're always eating because they have no teeth and no stomach so food passes through them quickly.

Unlike many animals, it is the male seahorse that carries the eggs.

A male seahorse can give birth to over 1,000 babies at a time. Not many babies survive and sometimes a male seahorse might eat its own babies.

STARFISH

STARFISH

Type: Invertebrate
Found: Oceans worldwide
Diet: Clams, oysters, coral and sponges

Starfish have an eye at the end of each arm. Each eye doesn't see much, but starfish can see all around them.

Most starfish have five arms, but some can have as many as 15!

To eat, a starfish pushes its stomach outside its mouth to start breaking down parts of its <u>prey</u>.

It makes a food soup that it can slurp up.

Starfish have no brain, no blood and no heart.

DOLPHIN

DOLPHIN
Type: Vertebrate (mammal)
Found: Oceans worldwide
Diet: Fish, octopuses and other mammals

Dolphins 'talk' to each other with clicks and whistles.

Dolphins have names. These are special sounds that are only used when 'talking' to that dolphin.

To make friends, dolphins will stroke each other with their fins.

Dolphins need to come to the surface of the water to breathe.

They breathe through the blowhole on top of their heads.

When they sleep, half their brain stays awake and they keep one eye open. This means they can always watch for danger.

OCTOPUS

OCTOPUS

Type: Invertebrate (mollusc)
Found: Worldwide
Diet: Molluscs and crustaceans

Octopuses shoot water out backwards to push them forwards. A jet engine does the same with air.

Octopuses can change colour. This helps them to hide or to warn other octopuses of danger.

Some types of octopus get up on two arms and run.

Giant Pacific octopuses are very smart. They can solve puzzles, open jars and even copy other octopuses.

Octopuses have three hearts and blue blood!

If an octopus is in danger, it can spray ink at a <u>predator</u>. This helps it to get away.

The suckers on an octopus's tentacles give the octopus a strong grip.

JELLYFISH

JELLYFISH
Type: Invertebrate
Found: Oceans worldwide
Diet: Ocean plants, crustaceans and small sea creatures

Jellyfish eat and poo through the same hole.

Jellyfish do not have a heart, brain or even eyes!

Many jellyfish don't swim but are moved around by the ocean.

Jellyfish disappear when they are washed up on the beach. They are mostly made of water and will eventually <u>evaporate</u> in the air.

If you cut some jellyfish in half, the pieces will grow into two new jellyfish.

WARNING
DON'T TOUCH A JELLYFISH ON THE BEACH, IT MIGHT BE ONE THAT STINGS.

Box jellyfish are deadly. One jellyfish could kill up to 60 people.

PISTOL SHRIMP

PISTOL SHRIMP

Type: Invertebrate (crustacean)

Found: Coral reefs in warm ocean waters

Diet: Other crustaceans

The pistol shrimp uses its one large claw to shoot a very fast and very hot bubble at its prey.

This bubble can travel as fast as a car and is loud enough to break glass.

PEACOCK MANTIS SHRIMP

PEACOCK MANTIS SHRIMP

Type: Invertebrate (crustacean)
Found: Warm waters in the Indian Ocean and Pacific Ocean
Diet: Crabs and molluscs

The peacock mantis shrimp has one of the fastest punches in the world for its size.

Its punch is as fast as a bullet. This lets the shrimp punch through the shells of its prey.

BLUE WHALE

BLUE WHALE

Type: Vertebrate (mammal)

Found: Oceans worldwide

Diet: Tiny ocean animals

The blue whale is the world's largest living creature. It is bigger than anything that has ever lived — even dinosaurs.

A blue whale can be bigger than a boat.

A blue whale's heartbeat can be heard over three kilometres away. That's because the heart is huge and weighs more than a cow.

They slow their heartbeat from around 35 beats per minute on the sea surface to two beats per minute when they're under water.

Like other whales, blue whales breathe through blowholes.

NARWHAL

A narwhal's horn is really a tooth. It grows upwards through its lip.

NARWHAL
Type: Vertebrate (mammal)
Found: Arctic waters
Diet: Fish and shellfish

The outside of the tusk is soft and sensitive. It's bendy at the end too.

All male narwhals grow a tusk but only a few females do.

Sometimes two narwhals cross tusks and rub them together to clean them.

Narwhals gather in groups of hundreds or even thousands.

Narwhals can break through ice if they need to come to the surface to breathe.

GLOSSARY

camouflaged	hidden by blending in with surroundings
crustaceans	animals that live in water and have a hard outer shell
diet	the kinds of food that a person or animal usually eats
evaporate	turn from a liquid into a gas or vapour, usually through heat
fish	an animal that lives in water and swims using fins and breathes with gills
invertebrates	animals that do not have a backbone inside their body
mammals	animals that are warm blooded, have a backbone and produce milk to feed their children
mollusc	a creature with a soft body, no backbone and usually a shell
predator	an animal that hunts other animals for food
prey	an animal that is eaten by another animal for food
temperate	a region or climate that has mild temperatures
vertebrate	an animal that has a backbone inside its body

INDEX

blood 11, 15
brains 11, 13, 16
breathing 13, 21, 23
crustaceans 5–8, 14, 16, 18–19

eating 8–9, 11, 16
eyes 10, 13, 16
females 22
males 9, 22

molluscs 5, 14, 19
shrimp 18–19
sleeping 13